Why People Move: Migration in African History

by
Philip D. Curtin

THE SIXTEENTH
𝕮𝖍𝖆𝖗𝖑𝖊𝖘 𝕰𝖉𝖒𝖔𝖓𝖉𝖘𝖔𝖓 𝕳𝖎𝖘𝖙𝖔𝖗𝖎𝖈𝖆𝖑 𝕷𝖊𝖈𝖙𝖚𝖗𝖊𝖘

Baylor University •Waco, Texas
March 7 & 8, 1994

MARKHAM PRESS FUND
WACO, TEXAS

This volume is the thirtieth volume published by the Markham Press Fund of Baylor University Press, established in memory of Dr. L. N. and Princess Finch Markham of Longview, Texas, by their daughters, Mrs. R. Matt Dawson of Waco, Texas, and Mrs. B. Reid Clanton of Longview, Texas.

The Charles Edmondson Historical Lecture Series, Number 16.

David W. Hendon, general editor.

Publication of this series of lectures is made possible by a special grant from Dr. E. Bud Edmondson of Longview, Texas.

Library of Congress Catalog Card Number: 95-77712
International Standard Book Number: 0-918954-61-4

Printed in the United States of America.

FOREWORD

In 1975 Dr. E. Bud Edmondson of Longview, Texas, began an endowment fund at Baylor University to honor his father, Mr. Charles S. B. Edmondson. Dr. Edmondson's intent was to have the proceeds from the fund used to bring to the University outstanding historians who could synthesize, interpret, and communicate history in such a way as to make the past relevant to the present generation.

Baylor University and the Waco community are grateful to Dr. Edmondson for his generosity in establishing the CHARLES EDMONDSON HISTORICAL LECTURES.

Professor Curtin, the sixteenth Edmondson Lecturer, presents a well-defined interpretation of why migration has occurred in Africa, highlighting numerous sociopolitical and socio-economic factors.

****

The views expressed in these lectures are those of the author and do not necessarily reflect the position of Baylor University or of the Markham Press Fund.

****

Although the Charles Edmondson Historical Lectures have been presented annually at Baylor University since 1978, they have not always been available for publication by the Markham Press Fund. A list of previous lectures appears at the end of this work.

3

MIGRATION IN EARLY AFRICAN HISTORY

Africa is an enormously diverse place. One of the assumptions left over from the cultural chauvinism of an earlier time is the belief that African diversity was a diversity of isolation—that Africans left in isolation had developed hundreds of ethnic units and languages, each of them having evolved pretty much on the spot where they now exist. Political commentators dwell on African "tribalism," as though age-old ethnic differences had emerged in the present century as a special African problem.

In fact, ethnic rivalries are not unknown elsewhere. The nineteenth century left us an over-simple view that people with similar heritage and appearance constitute "nations" that live together in blocs—that cultural diversity in a single society is unusual, and that the members of the nation should belong to a single nation-state. If such homogeneous nations ever existed, they were very rare, and one reason for their rarity is that people move around so much.

My objective in these two lecture is to look at patterns of human migration over the very long run, from the beginning of human existence down to the day before yesterday. Taking a single continent like Africa simplifies the problem of analyzing why people have moved from place to place and continue to move from place to place, more rapidly now than ever before.

Earliest Migrations Out of Africa

Let me go back to the beginning of African migration. In one sense all human migration was migration out of Africa. About 300,000 years ago, *Homo sapiens sapiens* first evolved in Africa, differentiated from a variety of other hominids.[1] It happened too long ago to be easily understood or understandable.

Over such a long time, many people left Africa to populate the rest of the world, and others certainly returned—part of an enormous, if unrecorded, population movement that must have taken place through many millennia of alternating ice ages and interglacial warm periods.

Linguistic evidence tells something about the probable course of these movements out of Africa; other evidence comes from patterns of biological evolution.[2] Geneticists have their own contribution, and more will no doubt some from the study of molecular biology. Meanwhile, Luigi Cavalli-Sforza and colleagues are pulling together a set of genetic maps based on more than a hundred individual heritable traits. Their *History and Geography of Human Genes* should be published later this year.[3]

Whether based on biology, genetics, or linguistics, these studies suggest that most of early human movement came from the success of a local population in achieving some technological breakthrough that made population growth and expansion possible. The invention of agriculture in the Middle East and the domestication of the horse on the Ukrainian steppe are examples.

Some early migrations in Africa, and with similar origins, began even before the invention of agriculture. About 15,000 years ago, people in Nubia or perhaps the Red Sea hills discovered techniques for the intensive collection of wild grains. The technique and the language of these people spread north into the Middle East and west across North Africa. This movement was not necessarily blanket or tidal, but it is safe to assume that the superior technology made possible population growth and migration into more sparsely settled territory— where the local people may well have picked up both the language and the technical skills of the immigrants.[4]

The evidence for this migration is both archaeological and linguistic, associated with the spread of Afro-Asiatic languages. That language family includes Arabic and Hebrew along with other, closely related Semitic languages of Ethiopia, like the classical Ge'ez and the later Amharic and Tigrinya. It also includes Ancient Egyptian, Berber, and the Chadic languages spoken in West Africa south of the Sahara. Linguists today

6

believe that this language family originated in Africa, probably somewhere in northern Ethiopian highlands or the Red Sea hills.

This hypothesis rests on reasoning sometimes called "the rule of least moves." If a large number of similar languages, about equally distant linguistically from one another, exist in a fairly confined region—as many different varieties of Afro-Asiatic languages do in the Horn of Africa—and if only a few of them are spoken today in distant places, it is easier to assume that a far off language group, like the Semitic languages, spread outward from the cluster, than to assume that all the clustered languages came from somewhere else. We know that Arabic moved into Africa only after the eighth century A.D., but this early movement may well have been the one that carried the Berber languages into the northwest corner of Africa. Similar reasoning is used in biology to determine the origin and diffusion of plant or animal species.[5]

Another major influence on early migration is changing climate. Until recently, the climatic record depended on indicators like the Nile floods or changes in the size of glaciers in Europe; but the pollen deposited in lakes and estuaries is an even better record going further back in time. Paleobotanists can now study these deposits through core samples from drillings in the bottoms of lakes and estuaries.

Historians have long known that the present aridity of the Sahara came into existence at about 2500 B.C., isolating sub-Saharan Africa from the main lines of change in the intercommunicating zones of Egypt and Mesopotamia—and later on from the Hellenic world of classical antiquity.

Recent research confirms that date for this most recent desiccation of the Sahara, but the climatic past is now known to have been far more complex, so complex that climatologists now set their studies in several different time scales. Change at one level took place within a century or so; at another level, over a millennium. Still other changes have to be plotted over several millennia. Northern Africa passed through a period of comparatively humid conditions from about 22,000 to 19,000 years ago, followed by extreme aridity about 16,000 to 13,000 years ago, with new periods of even greater humidity about 10,000 to 8,000 years ago and again at 6,000 years ago.[6] These changes have obvious long-term consequences for human migration, even though the patterns of migration are not yet clear in the archaeological record. People must have moved north into the present-desert region during humid periods, only to retreat when the arid millennia returned.

One population movement beginning about 10,000 years ago can be traced to a combination of newly humid conditions and new techniques to make use of them. The new technology was a complex of fishing and forms of land use for people living near water. Some archaeologists have called this an "aquatic civilization." This aquatic culture can be related to the present distribution of Nilo-Saharan languages, a movement presumably from the east, in what is now the Sudan Republic, westward through to the upper Benue in present-day Nigeria and north into the present Sahara north of Lake Chad—leaving the related Songhai even further west at the northern bend of the Niger isolated from the main body of Nilo-Saharan languages.[7]

Still another and far larger population movement in early Africa can be traced mainly through linguistic evidence. This is the movement of the Bantu-speaking people, who originally lived in the grasslands of Cameroon and neighboring parts of Nigeria, but who moved to occupy almost all of the great southern bulge of Africa. This was, again, a movement made possible by the technical superiority of Bantu-speakers over the dominantly hunting and gathering people who already occupied most of the great southern bulge of Africa. This movement is thought to have begun no earlier than about 3,000 B.C., based at first on the cultivation of cereals and yams, along with hunting and fishing. These Proto-Bantu-speakers also kept goats and made ceramics

The first phase of Bantu expansion took place along the border between forest and savanna, keeping to the same ecological zone their forefathers had lived in, the zone where their agricultural practices had been invented and worked best. Further advance to the south was slow, because it required an adaptation of their agricultural practices to the new conditions of the tropical forest, then to those of the forest-savanna mosaic south of the equator, still later to those of the dry woodland found still further south. It can be assumed that the advance of the language was mainly a migration of people, but it is also certain that the Bantu-speaking farmers assimilated many individuals from among the earlier, if sparser populations.

With the introduction of iron smelting about 500 B.C., this slow expansion—first west to east and then southward—began to change drastically. The precise entrance point for the early use of iron is unclear. It could have come from North Africa by one of several routes, or it could have been developed independently south of the Sahara. With iron smelting and improved techniques for cattle-keeping among the eastern Bantu-speakers, their expansion became more rapid, reaching the upper Zambezi valley about 200 B.C. and the Indian Ocean coast about 100 A.D. From that point a final phase was still more rapid, carrying the Bantu languages as far as northern Natal in South Africa by about 250 A.D. This whole process must have been far more complex than we now know, and it certainly absorbed many of the pre-Bantu inhabitants. The Nguni sub-group of Bantu languages, now the most southerly of all Bantu languages, picked up some elements from the Khoisan languages already spoken there, including three of the click sounds so characteristic of Khoisan. [8]

Though the Bantu migration was the most spectacular in these millennia, other, similar migrations can be traced through linguistic evidence. In each case, the speakers of the expanding language also possessed a new technique for food production that made for population growth and an advantage over the earlier inhabitants of the territory they came to occupy. This made possible the eastward expansion of the Ubanquian peoples from the vicinity of Lake Chad toward the Nile.[9] Or, in the first millennium of our era, innovations in pastoral technology helped people move south from the upper Nile into parts of present-day Uganda and Kenya.[10]

Early Movements into Africa

People also moved into Africa. About 1,000 B.C., seaborne migrations became more common in the world. The Inuit began their eastward movement from Siberia along the Arctic shores toward Greenland. The Polynesians also began their seaborne migration eastward into the Pacific in the first millennium B.C.[11]

9

A little after the Polynesians began moving east, the Malagasy, who also spoke an Austronesian language, moved west across the Indian Ocean from Indonesia to Madagascar, using maritime technology similar to that of the Polynesians, including double-hulled sailing vessels, a form of celestial navigation, and (perhaps most important of all) the habit of seeking new land for settlement. These voyages were not simply trading expeditions, with an all-male crew. They included women, plants, and domestic animals, so that newly discovered lands could be colonized.

Direct written evidence about the routes taken by these Malagasy voyages is missing, but two were possible. One was to sail directly west from Indonesia on the southeast trade winds; the other was to move north of the equator to catch the northeast trades, with the monsoon of the summer months providing an easy return. The northerly route was already known to mariners in Malaya and Sumatra, but the lack of evidence of Malagasy settlement in East Africa makes the southerly route seem more probable.[12] In any event, the Malagasy were the original settlers of Madagascar, and the Malagasy language is the dominant language on that island today, both for the those of Indonesian origin and for those whose ancestors migrated later from the African mainland.

The Muslim conquest of North Africa, beginning in the seventh century, linked the Maghrib more closely to the Middle East, but conquest alone was no migration. It probably involved even fewer than the estimated 80,000 or so Vandals who infiltrated the Roman empire and moved south through Spain to conquer Roman North Africa in the fifth century. The initial Arab armies and Arab garrisons were small compared to the existing urban populations in Egypt or the Maghrib. Indeed, by the time the Muslim invaders reached Spain, the armies themselves were mainly Berber-speaking people from North Africa, not Arabs from Arabia.

The more significant movement of populations into North Africa had different causes and different consequences. It began with the infiltration of Bedouins out of Arabia into the sedentary societies of the Middle East, continuing the drift of pastoral, Semitic-speaking people into the fertile crescent that had been chronic during the last two millennia B.C. Its origins seem to lie in the recurrent tendency of nomadic peoples to move into better-watered lands when they had the opportunity. They moved whenever population growth brought pressure on grazing land and disruption in sedentary societies made infiltration easy. William McNeill has called this tendency a "geographic gradient," moving nomadic peoples outward over centuries from such unfavorable and fragile climatic regions as Arabia and Mongolia.[13]

Arabs had begun to infiltrate the desert east of the Nile even before the Muslim era began, and the Bedouin movement continued afterwards as a sideshow to the more spectacular conquests of the early Umayyads. The Bedouin with their camels moved into an ecological niche that had not been fully occupied by Egyptians from the river valley. They infiltrated along the fringes of the irrigated lands, sometimes crossing into the western desert, with a gradual movement southward parallel to the Nile. The nomadic Beja of the Red Sea hills converted to Islam, but they held their own in their own territory; and they kept their Cushitic language into the twentieth century, even though the sedentary population of the Nile valley shifted to Arabic.[14]

Another nomadic drift out of Arabia stayed north of the desert. A little before about 1000 A.D., the Banu Hilal and Banu Sulaym of central Arabia moved into the Egyptian desert east of the Nile. Beginning about 1050, they moved west in force, not merely as nomads drifting on the fringe of sedentary civilization but also as raiders and occasional conquerors of sedentary states. Their westward drift continued for the next two centuries, until some of them reached the plains of Morocco. This Hilalian migration was not a truly massive movement of population. A usual estimate is that about a hundred thousand people left Arabia, but its influence was enormous. Some historians once blamed the Hilali for the destruction of the North African civilization that survived the decay of the Roman empire in Europe itself. While this view is probably exaggerated, the Hilalian passage through the Maghrib helped to complete the Arabization of Tunisia and to encourage the shift to

Arabic language among Berber-speakers in Algeria, Morocco, and the western Sahara.[15]

The cultural influence of any of these Arab migrations was far greater than the numbers involved might suggest. Present-day "Arabs" of the northern Sudan Republic speak Arabic, but the Arabian contribution to the gene pool of that region is usually estimated at only 15 or 20 percent. In the Maghrib, it was probably even less. Few as they were, however, these Arabian immigrants carried the prestige of Arabic as the language of God, expressed through the Koran. Without such migrants, Arabic might have spread to North Africa and the Sudan only as the language of religion and high culture—as it did to Muslim Spain or Persia.

Once south of the desert, some of these desert nomads made another ecological switch and turned to a pattern of transhumant semi-nomadic cattle-keeping along the southern desert edge. They came to be called *baqarra* in the Sudan. The opportunity was available because sedentary farmers south of the desert were tied to their fields during the three or four months of summer rain. Pastoral specialists, however, could take cattle north into the steppe where rainfall was enough to produce rich, if temporary, pasture from June into September. With the dry season, they could return to some base in the south with year-round water, where their cattle could live on dried grasses left from the rainy season. The Fulbe in West Africa filled a similar position of semi-nomadic transhumance, and they tended to drift eastward from the Senegal valley, just as the baqarra drifted west, until they met in the vicinity of Lake Chad.

These migrations were partly drawn forward by ecological opportunity, but they were also pushed by climatic variation. Periodic droughts lasting a few years to as much as a decade had been common along the desert fringe over recorded history. For transhumant pastoralists, these periodic droughts were like a demographic pump. A sequence of good years made for an increase in people and cattle alike. Then, when the rains failed, pastoralists could move south away from the desert in search of a better dry-season base. Once the drought was over, they moved north again, but not necessarily to their old wet-season pasture.

12

The Basis of Early Slave Migrations

Slavery and the slave trade entered into African migrations a little after the fifth century A.D., when camels first became available in the Sahara and North Africa. Camel caravans changed the Sahara from a barrier to trade and communication into a relatively easy north-south route, largely because camels were the most efficient form of land transportation available at the time.[16] The numbers are uncertain, but some flow of slaves from tropical Africa into the Mediterranean basin and Arabia had begun by the seventh century.[17]

Slavery, however, was much less important in Islamic North Africa than it had been in Roman times. Islamic social forms were a direct descendent of Roman patterns, but the Muslim societies no longer employed slaves as agricultural labor on a large scale, with occasional exceptions like the use of black slaves—presumably from Africa—in irrigation and drainage works in southern Iraq in the eighth and ninth centuries. The more common institutional pattern, sometimes called Muslim service slavery, replaced the Roman pattern of latifundia. Slaves were valued less for their labor than for the fact that they were aliens, who could be placed most usefully in occupations better left to strangers. One of these was domestic service of a particularly intimate sort, including concubines, eunuchs as harem guards, and women held for prostitution.[18]

Another occupation best left to strangers was military service and certain administrative functions, even those of considerable importance. A ruler could better trust a slave, his own property, than members of the local society with kinship ties and personal interests different from his own. Slave armies were common in the Muslim world—in Ottoman Turkey, in Egypt, and in Morocco, where slave soldiers from across the Sahara were used extensively in the eighteenth century. Because these slaves were valued as strangers, that value declined after the first generation, and successors had to be recruited beyond the frontiers of Islam; but comparatively few of these recruits came from Africa. Byzantine Christians and other Christian war prisoners were one source. The Caucasus mountain region was another. Still another, perhaps the most important of all, was

13

the plains of the Ukraine and other Slavic regions north of the Black Sea.[19] That region had been a major source of slaves for the Roman world, and it once again became an important source for the Mediterranean between the twelfth century and the fifteenth. It was at this period that the Medieval Latin word, *slavus,* identifying Slavs as slaves, came into common use, with cognates in several European languages and in Arabic.

In these same centuries, slaves from across the Sahara began to be important in North Africa, with some spill-over into Mediterranean Europe. The traffic began in the first centuries of Islamic control over North Africa,[20] but the size of the movement is a continuing puzzle for historians. The contemporaneous estimates are far too large for the apparent present-day influence of sub-Saharan Africans in the North African gene pool, especially so because this traffic is reported to have included a large proportion of women.[21]

The importance of places like sub-Saharan Africa and Ukraine as sources of slaves over several centuries raises an important question for the world history of migration. Why did some societies seemingly serve as recurrent sources of slaves for export, while others were chronic importers? Among the exporting regions were tropical Africa, Ukraine, Circasia, some regions in India and south China—at least for the quasi-slave-trade in indented labor in the nineteenth century. Speculative explanations have sometimes stressed overpopulation, especially for India and China; but the slave-furnishing regions of tropical Africa were certainly not over-populated to the same extent.

In now seems clear that warfare in much of western tropical Africa included the convention that the entire conquered population could be legitimately enslaved—not just the combatant war prisoners. This in turn made the capture of the opposing population a major military objective—in contrast to the more common European effort to defeat the enemy's army in the field or to seize enemy territory.

It tropical Africa, this military objective encouraged an internal slave trade. Women and children could sometimes be reduced to servitude and kept within the victorious society, but young male adults were too dangerous to keep around. In later centuries, such captives were often sold to merchants who followed the armies. A hundred miles or more from the scene of capture, they might be sold to a new society more capable of absorbing them, and the chance of a successful escape would be less. Young men of military age might often be fitted into the purchasers' own fighting force. The prevalence of these patterns of capture and commercialization of prisoners meant that slaves were available for an export trade as well, once North Africans appeared on the desert edge or Europeans appeared on the coast.[22]

These patterns of enslavement were related in turn to other aspects of society in west tropical Africa. Control over land was rarely transferable by purchase. Low levels of population density might have contributed to this pattern, in the sense that land, being plentiful, earned no rent.[23] John Thornton has recently pointed out that population densities were not nearly low enough to have that consequence in most of tropical Africa. In his view, slavery was prevalent because slaves were the most readily available form of revenue-producing property recognized by African law. In the traditions of Medieval Europe, land was key to productive capability, and ownership of land often included the control over a labor force to work it. In contemporaneous Africa, land was owned, but it was owned corporatively by kinship groups or by the state. It was not always plentiful, but it was readily available at a low price or no price to those who could make use of it—that is, to those who owned the labor to work it.[24] In Europe, then, land ownership tended to imply easy control over labor, while in Africa ownership of labor tended to make for easy control over land.[25]

Plantations and the Atlantic Encounter

The most important and spectacular emigration from Africa was the Atlantic slave trade, probably the largest intercontinental movement of people before the nineteenth century. It began a little before 1450 and lasted more than four centuries, to about 1870. It was not equally important during all of those centuries, but its association with the plantation complex in the tropical Americas made it one of the central aspects of the world economy from the 1670s to the 1840s.[26]

15

This new migration grew out of three independent developments in world history. The first was the existing pattern of warfare and enslavement in tropical western Africa, which was to make slaves available for sale on the African coast once European buyers appeared. The other two were on the demand side. One was the ancient pattern of using the slave trade to concentrate people for new enterprises. The other was the demographic consequences of new contact across the Atlantic.

Before the industrial revolution, the vast majority of any human population had to work at food production and preparation. This need required an even distribution of human population, with the size of that population adjusted to the availability of land and technology. A new enterprise like a mine or a plantation needed new concentrations people, since the people already present were necessarily busy with other, existing tasks. The newcomers had to be drawn in as migrants from a distance. In the absence of an organized labor market, the usual way to recruit migrants was by purchase. In Periclean Athens, for example, comparatively few slaves worked the land, but an estimated 15 to 30 percent of the slave population worked the silver mines at Laurion.[27] Early sugar plantations were equally labor-intensive and required people from a distance. As early as the eighth century, some sugar plantations in Mesopotamia had used African slaves.[28]

When Europeans borrowed Muslim sugar technology to create plantations in the Levant during the crusades, they too turned to the slave trade to meet their need for labor—though not yet from Africa. Africans began to appear toward the end of the fifteenth century, imported to work new sugar plantations on the Atlantic islands like Madeira and the Canaries. After 1453, the Turkish capture of Constantinople reduced access to the old source of slaves at the Black Sea ports, and the west coast of Africa was much closer to the new plantations.

The Columbus quincentennary attracted public attention to the importance of "the encounter" between Europe and the Americas, but it also created a false emphasis. The maritime encounters of the fifteenth century involved three continents— Europe, tropical Africa, and the Americas—not just two of these.

16

In fact, the main breakthrough in maritime technology took place on the coast of Africa, roughly a half-century before Columbus's voyage. European mariners who wanted to sail west faced a problem in the existing wind patterns. Prevailing winds in northern Europe blew from the west, while in southern Europe they blew still more strongly and regularly from the northeast—favorable for an outward passage, but too strong for an easy return. In the European Middle Ages, it had been safe enough in summer to explore at sea to the northwest—say to Iceland, or even Greenland—and the prevailing westerlies assured the possibility of a return.

The northeast trades were different. They blew all year round, and they set up a southwesterly current along the Moroccan and Saharan coasts. With the ships available in the fifteenth century and earlier, it was hard enough to make way against an unfavorable wind by tacking. With an opposing current of a half-knot to a knot and a half, like that off the Saharan coast, it was nearly impossible. That was why sailors' talk sometimes told of ships that set out to the southwest and fell off the edge of the earth.

In about the 1440s, anonymous Portuguese mariners solved the problem of a return from the southwest. They first discovered that the winds along the Saharan coast were variable according to the time of day—more on-shore in the daytime and more off-shore at night. That discovery made it possible to tack laboriously back up the coast. The most important breakthrough, however, came when someone discovered that long tack to the northwest, sailing as close as possible to the northeast trades, would carry a ship north to the belt of prevailing westerlies that began just north of the Azores. A return to Portugal from that point would be simple.[29]

With that discovery, it was possible to reach any coastal point in west or west-central Africa, and to return with comparative ease. The Portuguese began to build their castle at Elmina in 1481, established diplomatic relations with Kongo and Benin, and began to establish sugar plantations as far away as São Tomé by 1493. What these Portuguese mariners had done was to discover the north Atlantic portion of the world wind system. Knowing how to return from West Africa meant that they also

17

knew that a ship sailing west in the latitude of the Canaries could easily return in latitudes north of the Azores. That is, of course, precisely what Columbus did, and he already had the experience of a voyage to the Gold Coast and back to learn the wind patterns.

From these beginnings, Africa continued as an important part of an Atlantic triangle. European mariners provided the technology, and European monarchs claimed the conquered territory in the New World, but it was African, not European, diseases that depopulated the American tropics, and, in any decade before the 1840s, it was Africans who provided the vast majority of migrants across the Atlantic.

The depopulation of the humid tropics in the Americas began with smallpox, carried by illicit African slave imports to Hispaniola in 1517. Falciparum malaria and yellow fever followed. These three depopulated the tropical lowlands of the Caribbean islands and mainland, northeast Brazil, and the Amazon basin—with an assist from other, European diseases, though those played a more important role in North America and the South American highlands.[30] A few Indian survivors contributed to the gene pool of the later Caribbean, but, except for scattered mixed groups like the Caribs, Indian communities disappeared.

Ironically, the same diseases that killed off the American Indians made Africans the ideal population to take their place. Most people in West Africa had acquired an apparent immunity to falciparum malaria. They usually had an acquired immunity to yellow fever, which is far less fatal to children than to those who first encounter it as adults. Africans were less immune to pneumonia than Europeans were at that period, but the death rate of newly arrived Africans in the American tropics was usually a quarter or less that of newly arrived Europeans.[31]

The scene was set by natural epidemiological conditions that might well have made a massive migration across the tropical Atlantic a foregone conclusion. That was the outcome, but it was not automatic. Africans had no incentive to migrate, even if the full horrors of plantation slavery were hidden from them. The incentives that set the slave trade in motion operated on the rulers and mercantile élites in Africa and in Europe—not on the people who actually made the trip or manned the ships that carried them.

Those incentives depended in turn on still another set of technological changes. The sugar plantation complex, which had already moved from its early home in the Levant to the Atlantic islands before 1492, moved on to Brazil in the second half of the sixteenth century, to the Lesser Antilles in the seventeenth, and on to the Greater Antilles and the Guianas in the eighteenth.[32] During this sequence, sugar plantations passed through a series of technological changes that made sugar production cheaper. Cheap sugar was reflected in rising European consumption of a product with a high price-elasticity of demand.

The cheaper sugar came partly from new economies of scale, partly from better machinery for grinding and refining cane, partly from improved maritime technology that made it possible to move high-bulk, low-value cargoes of people and goods across thousands of miles. The sugar, the slaves, Indian textiles to pay for them on the African coast, and the salt fish to feed them were all carried by sailing ships—the most efficient and most important source of non-human, non-animal power before the invention of the steam engine. The technical innovations that counted most, however, were commercial practices that made possible the mature plantation complex—the first economic system anywhere in the world to import such a high proportion of its inputs—including labor—and to export such a large proportion of its outputs over inter-continental distances.

These changed commercial practices were not those of Europeans alone. The Indian textile industry responded with rising quantities of cloth for sale on the African coast. The west and west-central African trading partners built a sophisticated commercial system capable, by the eighteenth century, of delivering an annual average of more than 50,000 people for sale on the coast. In the peak year, it delivered more than 80,000.[33]

This forced migration grew through time. Around 42,000 people left Africa in the fifteenth century, bound almost entirely for Europe and the Atlantic islands. In the sixteenth century,

325,000 left Africa, mainly for Brazil and Spanish America. In the seventeenth, the total had risen to 1.9 million. In the eighteenth century and on to 1809, when the legal trade began to be cut off, 6.7 million left, with the Caribbean now the most important destination. Between 1810 and the end of the trade about 1870, a further 2.6 million left, with Cuba and Brazil now the main destinations.[34]

The sheer size of this migration raises an important interpretive question. How was this movement of people related to the industrial revolution that was soon to mark such an important watershed in human history? The slave trade was partly an extension of pre-industrial patterns, like the earlier non-African slave trade that served to concentrate people for mining or plantations. It was partly an extension of African traditions of warfare and enslavement, and it contained some aspects of Muslim service slavery. With time, however, new levels of size and complexity made it a substantially different institution. A dividing line can be drawn in the second half of the seventeenth century, marking a change in scale, the entry of new participants, and the application of new technologies of commerce and transportation.

In the first half of the seventeenth century, the levels of slave imports from Africa into Europe and the Americas had stabilized at about 7,500 a year. By the last quarter of that century, the annual average had risen to more than 24,000, and it nearly doubled to reach 43,000 in the first two decades of the eighteenth century.[35] The late seventeenth century was also the time when the English, Dutch, and French became major carriers, and when the central destination in the Americas shifted from Brazil and the Spanish Caribbean to the Antilles. With these changes, the plantation complex came to be more closely integrated with the centers of economic and technological change in Europe itself.

Economic historians in recent decades have been pushing the earliest signs of the industrial revolution into the earlier eighteenth century and even into the seventeenth.[36] This change in timing weakens an older interpretation that considered the eighteenth-century apogee of the plantation complex to be a pre-industrial phenomenon about to be swept away by the advance of capitalist industrialism in the nineteenth century. It is not necessary to include the plantation complex as *part of* the industrial revolution to see it as a dynamic aspect of the world economy in the eighteenth century and one closely related to the economic and technological changes leading toward the industrial revolution.

These changes, however, were transitional. The early era of the slave trade clearly belongs to the pre-industrial world, while the eighteenth-century trade was somehow a build-up toward the industrial age that was to come. By the nineteenth century, the industrial age was under way, with enormous changes for the kinds of migration that were to take place into, within, and out of Africa, and I will turn to these changed conditions in the next lecture.

Notes to Lecture I

1. For a recent review of the controversies over the evolution of early humans see Roger Lewin, *The Origin of Modern Humans* (New York: W. H. Freeman, 1993).
2. A recent example would be Jonathan Kingdon, *Self-Made Man: Human Evolution from Eden to Extinction* (New York: John Wiley, 1993).
3. Luigi Luca Cavalli-Sforza and others, *History and the Georgraphy of Human Genes* (Princeton, NJ: Princeton University Press, forthcoming). Some of the main lines are foreshadowed in Cavalli-Sforza, "Genes, Peoples and Languages," *Scientific American*, 265 (1991), 104-110, and Cavalli-Sforza, Paolo Menozzi, and Alberto Piazza, "Demic Expansions and Human Evolution," *Science*, 259 (1993), 639-46.
4. Christopher Ehret, "On the Antiquity of Agriculture in Ethiopia," *Journal of African History*, 20 (1979), 161-77.
5. For the application of the principle of least moves to African linguistic history see Christopher Ehret and Merrick Posnansky, *The Archaeological and Linguistic Reconstruction of African History* (Berkeley: University of California Press, 1982), 12-13.
6. Roderick J. Macintosh, "The Pulse Model: Genesis and Accommodation of Specialization in the Middle Niger," *Journal of African History*, 34 (1993), 181-220; George E. Brooks, "A Provisional Historical Schema for Western Africa Based on Seven Climate Periods (c. 9,000 B.C. to the 19th Century)," *Cahiers d'études africaines*, 26 (1986), 432-63; Alfred Muzzolini, "Les climats du Sahara et sur ses bordures, du Pleistocène final à l'aride actuel," *Empuries*, 47 (1985), 8-27.
7. J. E. G. Sutton, "The Aquatic Civilization of Middle Africa," *Journal of African History*, 15 (1974), 527-46; Ehret and Posnansky, *Archaeological and Linguistic Reconstruction*, esp. 7-10.
8. For a recent summary of these movements see Jan Vansina, chapter one in Philip D. Curtin, Steven

Feierman, Leonard Thompson, and Jan Vansina, *African History*, 2nd ed. (London: Longman, 1995).

9. A. B. L. Stemler, J. R. Harland, and J. M. J. Dewet, "Caudatum Sorghums and Speakers of Chari-Nile Languages in Africa," *Journal of African History*, 16 (1975), 161-83; Douglas E. Saxon, "Linguistic Evidence for the Eastward Spread of Ubangian Peoples," in Ehret and Posnansky, *Archaeological and Lingistic Reconstrucion*, 66-77.

10. Christopher Ehret, *Southern Nilotic History: Linguistic Approaches to the Study of the Past* (Evanston: Northwestern University Press, 1971).

11. Irving Rouse, *Migrations in Prehistory: Inferring Population Movements from Cultural Remains* (New Haven: Yale University Press, 1986).

12. F. Ramiandrasoa, *Atlas historique du peuplement de madagascar* (Antananarivo: Université de Madagascar, Académie Malgache, 1975); B. Domenichini-Ramiaramanana, "Madagascar," in UNESCO, *General History of Africa*, 8 vols. (London: Heinemann, 1988), 3, 681-703.

13. William H. McNeill, *The Rise of the West: A History of the Human Community* (Chicago: University of Chicago Press, 1963), 484-94; and "Human Migration in World Perspective," *Population and Development Review*, 10 (1984), 4-5.

14. Yusuf Fadl Hassan, *The Arabs and the Sudan from the Seventh to the Early Sixteenth Century* (Edinburgh: Edinburgh University Press, 1967); Richard W. Bulliet, *The Camel and the Wheel* (New York: Columbia University Press, 1975), 114-124.

15. Humphrey J. Fisher, "The Eastern Maghrib and the Central Sudan," in Roland Oliver (Ed.), *Cambridge History of Africa* (Cambridge: Cambridge University Press, 1977) 3, 243-45.

16. William H. McNeill, "The Eccentricity of Wheels, or Eurasian Transportation in Historical Perspective," *American Historical Review*, 92 (1987), 1111-26; Bulliet, *The Camel and the Wheel*, 111-40.

17. Ralph A. Austen, "The Trans-Saharan Slave Trade: A Tentative Census," in Henry A. Gemery and Jan S.

Hogendorn (Eds.), *The Uncommon Market: Essays in the Economic History of the Atlantic Slave Trade* (New York: Academic Press, 1979), 23-76.

18. Phillips, *Slavery*, 66-87.
19. For Muslim military slavery see Patricia Crone, *Slaves on Horses: The Evolution of an Islamic Polity* (New York: Cambridge University Press, 1980); Daniel Pipes, *Slave Soldiers and Islam: The Genesis of a Military System* (New Haven, CT: Yale University Press, 1981).
20. Elizabeth Savage, "Berbers and Blacks: Ibadi Slave Traffic in Eighth-Century North Africa," *Journal of African History*, 33 (1992), 351-68.
21. J.O. Hunwick, "Black Africans in the Mediterranean," *Slavery & Abolition*, 13 (1993), 25-27. Elizabeth Savage (Ed.), *The Human Commodity: Perspectives on the Trans-Saharan Slave Trade* (London: Frank Cass, 1992) reviews the recent scholarship concerning this trade. Also published as volume 12, no. 1 of *Slavery & Abolition* (April 1992).
22. John K. Thornton, *Africa and Africans in the Making of the Atlantic World, 1400-1680* (New York: Cambridge University Press, 1992), 72-97.
23. Jack Goody, *Tradition, Technology, and the State* (London: Oxford University Press, 1971), 21-38.
24. Thornton, *Africa and Africans*, 74-79.
25. These conditions in Africa of the fifteenth and sixteenth centuries bear some resemblance to the evolution of slavery in Muscovy over those same centuries, leading in the Muscovite case to the change-over from slavery to a system of serfdom attached to the land. The major region of slave supply to the Mediterranean basin at that time was, however, south of Muscovy proper and drew to some degree on captured Muscovites. Richard Hellie, *Slavery in Russia: 1450-1725* (Cambridge: Harvard University Press, 1982), 1-26.

A long discussion of the relationship between land scarcity and labor control through slavery or other means goes back at least as far as Herman Merivale, *Lectures on Colonization and Colonies Delivered before the University of Oxford in 1839, 1840, & 1841*, 2nd ed. (London, 1861), and comes down through H. J. Nieboer, *Slavery as an Industrial System* (The Hague: Martinus Nijhoff, 1910), and Evsey Domar to Orlando Patterson.

26. For the role of the plantation complex in world history see Philip D. Curtin, *The Rise and Fall of the Plantation Complex* (New York: Cambridge University Press, 1990).

27. Kingsley Davis, "The Migration of Human Populations," *Scientific American*, 23 (1974), 95.

28. Phillips, *Slavery*, 79.

29. Raymond Mauny, *Les navigations médiévales sur les côtes sahariennes antérieures à la découverte portugaises (1434)* (Lisbon, 1960).

30. Philip D. Curtin, "Disease Exchange Across the Tropical Atlantic," *History and Philosophy of the Life Sciences*, 15 (1993), 169-96.

31. Philip D. Curtin, "Epidemiology and the Slave Trade," *Political Science Quarterly,* 83 (1968), 190-216.

32. Curtin, *The Plantation Complex, passim.*

33. Philip D. Curtin, *The Atlantic Slave Trade: A Census* (Madison: University of Wisconsin Press, 1969). The data have been greatly modified in detail, but the main lines are reasonably accurate for the whole period. For recent revision see David Richardson, "Slave Exports from West and West-Central Africa, 1700-1810: New Estimates: Volume and Distribution," *Journal of African History*, 30 (1989), 1-22.

34. Paul Lovejoy, *Transformations in Slavery: A History of Slavery in Africa* (New York: Cambridge University Press, 1983), 19, 47, 141; Richardson, "Slave Exports," 10.

35. Curtin, *Census*, 119, 216, 266.

36. John Komlos, "Thinking about the Industrial Revolution," *Journal of European Economic History*, 18 (1989), 191-206.

LECTURE II

AFRICAN MIGRATION IN THE INDUSTRIAL AGE

My second lecture on African migration has to do with new patterns that emerged with and following the industrial revolution in Europe. Let me begin, however, with a bigger picture of migration in the tropical world since the Atlantic encounter. Africa was sometimes involved and sometimes not, but to understand what happened in Africa, it is important to know the larger patterns.

First, major movement, as we saw last time, was the repeopling of the Americas after the death of the Indians in the tropical lowlands. Africans made the largest contribution through the eighteenth century, but some European migrants were also involved.

Second, after about the 1840s, came the mass movement overseas of the Europeans. In the process they created the neo-Europes of the Americas, Australia, New Zealand, with important population movements across the Urals into Siberia. This spread of Europeans was even larger than the Atlantic slave trade had been.

Third, in the tropical world, beginning with the nineteenth century and continuing to the 1920s, Indians and Chinese replaced Africans as the most important group of long-distance migrants. Some went to the American tropics, but the plantation complex expanded beyond its old center in the American tropics. Some of the Asian migrants went to Cuba, Trinidad, and Guyana, but even more went to places as diverse as Malaysia, Thailand, Hawaii, Fiji, Peru, Cuba, and Australia.

Finally, in the second half of the twentieth century, tropical migrants began to move into the developed world—West Indians into Britain, Algerians into France, Turks to Germany, Pakistanis to the Persian Gulf, Mexicans into the United States.

Africans had some part in these movements, but for African migration at large, the important fact was that the export slave trade came to an end.[1] The growing flow of more-or-less coerced, indentured, or shanghaied migrants from India and China replaced forced migration from Africa. It is not necessary here to be concerned with *how much* these new currents of labor migration were like the slave trade they replaced. *Some* coercion took place at the point of recruitment, but the terms of indenture normally stated that the contract could be sold to a third party without the worker's consent and that failure to work as directed in the country of destination was punishable by imprisonment at hard labor. That was coercion enough.[2]

These new sources and new destinations are at the core of world migration in the nineteenth century. In sheer numbers, this new migration far exceeded the size of the slave trade. In 1883 and 1884 alone, Singapore received an annual average of 112,000 immigrants from China, though not necessarily under indenture.[3] That alone was more than the whole of the Atlantic slave trade in its peak year. Africa was, however, on the fringes of these new migrations, both as source and as destination; and the end of the export slave trade did not end the movement of enslaved people within Africa, as we will see presently.

Migrants into Southern Africa

South Africa began to participate in some of these new patterns as early as the seventeenth century, though only in a small way. The earliest European immigrants were part of a world-wide pattern of European trade diasporas that spread along the sea lanes of the Indian Ocean and South China Sea beginning in the sixteenth century and reached South Africa only in the seventeenth.[4] The Cape of Good Hope was a natural way-station for that trade. It had good harbors on either side of Table Mountain and a fertile, Mediterranean climate in the hinterland. The Portuguese had placed small settlements in southern Africa at various times, but the Khoikhoi had driven them off. The Dutch Vereenigte Oost-Indische Compagnie (VOC) established a new settlement in 1652 and fortified it with Cape Town Castle at the foot of Table Mountain.

Cape Town's intended function was like that of European

posts serving the slave trade in West Africa. At the Cape settlement, no more than a thousand Europeans were present at any time before the 1680s—hardly enough to figure as significant immigration—but the disease environment of the Cape of Good Hope was unusually favorable to European residents, while that of tropical posts was remarkably unfavorable. Then, in 1679, the VOC decided to make the Cape more nearly self-supporting by encouraging settlers called free burghers who were not on its payroll but might be called out for militia duty, and who would produce food for the garrison and for sale to passing ships. From 1679 to 1707, the VOC sought to build up population through assisted immigration of German, Dutch, or French Protestants. In all, it sent out some 1,630 people.

Though European settlers were few, their population growth was so rapid that the demographic consequences were *like* those of a stream of immigrants. By 1707, the European population consisted of about 700 VOC employees and 2,000 free burghers.[5] After that date, the VOC no longer encouraged immigration, and the flow died to a trickle; but the sex-ratio soon became normal, and the population began to increase, until its descendants grew to become the main constituent of a white Afrikaans-speaking population of nearly three million in South Africa today. (Much the same thing happened at the French trading base at the mouth of the Saint Lawrence, where an initial input of less than 10,000 settlers grew into the French Canadian population of more than five million.)

The recent racial domination of South Africa by overseas Europeans has tended to obscure the fact that the VOC introduced far more migrants from Africa and Asia than from Europe. Slavery was common in the plantation sphere of the Americas and also on Java, where the Dutch had their principal Southeast Asian base. It was therefore logical for the company to import slaves, and the free burghers also used coercion to obtain labor from their Khoikhoi and San neighbors. The form of slavery at the Cape, however, was a mixture of the plantation model common to the West Indies and the African model, where slaves were found in many different occupations, of which field labor was only one.

29

Through the whole period of legal slave imports, up to the early nineteenth century, the VOC brought in a total of 65,000 slaves, of whom 26 percent were from the African mainland, mostly from eastern Africa. Another 26 percent were from India. Twenty-three percent came from Indonesia, and 25 percent from Madagascar. It is likely that each of these four segments was larger than the total emigration from Europe over this same period.[6]

The demographic results were different, however. A combination of unfavorable sex-ratios, disease, and low standards of living kept the imported slaves from multiplying as rapidly as the European settlers did. Their descendants, with some genetic contribution from the Dutch and Khoikhoi, nevertheless are the "coloured" population of South Africa today, a community only slightly larger than the Afrikaans-speaking whites.

The English-speaking segment of the present South African population was more clearly an aspect of European industrial expansion. When Great Britain secured the Cape Colony in 1805, its objectives were much the same as those of the VOC—a way-station on the route to India. A small flow of immigrants began to arrive as early as the 1820s, growing much larger after the discovery of diamonds in the 1850s and of gold in the 1880s. The earliest source was Great Britain, but many came from continental Europe as well after the 1890s. Almost all assimilated to the English rather than the Afrikaner community and joined to form the basis for the English-home-language population of nearly 2 million in South Africa today.

Settler immigration was also important in Algeria, where the French conquest began in 1830 and ended about 1872. As in South Africa, the European immigrants and their descendants became a significant minority with dominant power and wealth, but the *colons*—coming from Spain and Malta as well as from France—rose to be only about 11 percent of the total before the war for Algerian independence.[7] After the war, the vast majority emigrated to Europe.

A final group of European settlers came from Portugal, which sponsored European emigration to its African colonies as a national policy during much of the period before the coup of

1975 brought independence to lusophone Africa. As of 1956, Europeans made up 2.5 percent of the Angolan population and 1.1 percent of the population of Mozambique. These are not enormous numbers, but the proportion are higher than that found anywhere in British or French colonies in tropical Africa other than the Rhodesias and Nyasaland.[8]

Nineteenth-century Transitions in Southern Africa

Military innovations also entered the South African pattern of migration in the early nineteenth century, when two separate but parallel tactical changes led to widespread migration and demographic change. Technological innovation had often encouraged migration in the past, but the innovation was usually an improved means of production. These innovations were new means of destruction. One was the creation of a new military system among the Nguni people of Natal. The other was secondary empire building based on Western weapons and tactics, but beyond European political control.

The Nguni military innovation led to the Mfecane—the outbreak of widespread warfare that accompanied the rise of a Zulu state. The precise origins of the movement and the character of Shaka, the principal Zulu leader, are much contested by historians. The nature of the new military system is clear, though it remains uncertain who first put it into use. It consisted of disciplined infantry formations with some similarities to Roman legionaries or Swiss pikemen of sixteenth-century Italian wars. These units fought with a short stabbing spear and shield in a formation that kept the mass of the force in the center, with horn-like wings on either side to advance and surround an enemy.

These disciplined units, called *impi*, were based on the African institution of the age-grade, the social unit consisting of all young men initiated at the same time. By bringing an entire age-grade into a standing army as a unit, the Zulu achieved a high degree of discipline and esprit de corps. By the 1820s, the Zulu and others who used the new military system could usually win out against those who had not yet adopted it.

The new system thus gave an advantage only to those who directed aggression outward against more distant peoples where the new tactics were still unknown. The system therefore led to aggressive migration outward from the heartland of the Nguni culture in central and northern Natal. Some of these military migrations were those of refugees, the defeated fleeing from the warfare in Natal, but taking the new military system with them. Others were simply the work of opportunists who saw an opening in which to build their own power or that of their group.

The movement and counter-movement was complex, but the main lines can be simplified into a leapfrog pattern. One leader moved north into what is now Swaziland and founded the Swazi kingdom. Another passed still further north to found another kingdom in what is now southern Mozambique. Others went further still and founded a series of small kingdoms in central and southern Tanzania, where their descendants still live as the Angoni, after the Nguni language of their original homeland.

Other offshoots of the Mfecane crossed the Drakensberg onto the high veld of what is now the Orange Free State and Transvaal. One leader in northern Transvaal attracted a following that was partly Nguni and partly local. That group became the Ndebele, who moved further northwest into western Zimbabwe, where their descendants still live. Another offshoot of the Mfecane, the Kololo, moved out further still and conquered the Lozi kingdom on the upper Zambezi in present-day Zambia. There, the Lozi and Kololo cultures merged to form the political and cultural entity that became, in the colonial period, Barotseland in Northern Rhodesia.

The parallel migration with military roots was the northward movement of the Afrikaans-speaking overseas Europeans from the Cape Colony. "Secondary empire" is a term commonly used by historians of nineteenth-century Africa to describe military aggression and political aggrandizement on the part of local people beyond European political control. These empires were secondary in the sense that their power was based on the technological achievements of Europe. The Cape Afrikaners in the early nineteenth century had developed their own new military system based on mounted infantry armed with muskets. The Xhosa they confronted across their eastern frontier used the same military methods, but the Mfecane made it possible for the Cape farmers using those methods to move west of the Xhosa and then north onto the high veld, where their tactics could usually defeat the impi. They established their own political and military dominance over the districts already disrupted by the Mfecane and founded a number of new political entities beyond British control, of which the two Boer republics of the Orange Free State and Transvaal lasted longest. The overseas European migrants remained a minority among the African populations they came to dominate, but they maintained a troubled independence from Europe until the British conquest at the end of the century.

Slavery and Secondary Empire in Tropical Africa

By the early nineteenth century, the pattern of secondary empire began to emerge in tropical Africa as well, just when the Atlantic slave trade was drawing to an end. It was a confused period, when new leadership emerged and new state building changed the political map right across the Western Sudan from Senegambia to Lake Chad. Some new political units, like the Sokoto Caliphate of northern Nigeria, had no apparent connection to events in industrializing Europe; but other religious revolutions that followed after the mid-century include aspects of secondary-empire-building. In the 1850s and 1860s, Sheikh Umar Tal created a new empire with a Muslim ideological base. It stretched along the southern desert-edge and savanna country from the upper Senegal and the Niger. Samori Turé built another new empire, even more clearly based on European arms, along the forest-savanna fringe from the sources of the Niger across the present-day Côte d'Ivoire and ultimately into the northern part of present-day Ghana.

Extensive migration accompanied this secondary-empire-building—and not just the marching of armies. Umar Tal attracted a broad following from the Fulbe people of the Senegal valley, partly as military followers but also as settlers in the lands he conquered.[9] Samori's conquests also involved the movement of conquering migrants, and of refugees who fled ahead of his armies. All this military activity brought about an enormous increase in the number of slaves captured and sold into the trade—just at a time when the Atlantic slave trade was cut off. The result was a massive shift of population throughout West Africa, a shift that has only recently begun to be studied. The proportion of slaves in the population of the Western Sudan at the beginning of the nineteenth century is not known, but, at the moment of European conquest in the 1880s and later, it was commonly in the range of 50 to 70 percent.[10]

The pattern was similar in the eastern Sudan. In the 1820s, Muhammad 'Ali of Egypt created the first secondary empire with the conquest of the Nubia and the Nilotic Sudan down to the frontiers of Ethiopia. One incentive was his need for slave soldiers in the Egyptian army, and one result was to increase the pace of enslavement all across the savanna from Lake Chad to the Red Sea and up the Nile into the Bahr al-Ghazal.[11] The resulting population movements were as massive here as in West Africa, perhaps greater than the slave movements at any earlier period in African history, but the precise size and destinations of all these enslaved people may be beyond the possibility of accurate reconstruction.

The Slave Trade and Coerced Labor in Eastern Africa

In East Africa, the nineteenth-century pattern of enslavement and slave trade was both different and similar. Historians of Africa sometimes draw a sharp distinction between the end of the export trade in slaves from West Africa and the continued slave exports from the east through most of the nineteenth century. In fact the main difference was that the slaves moving in East Africa were often moved by sea up the coast to Kenya or Zanzibar, or offshore to islands like Madagascar or the Mascarenes, while slaves in West Africa moved overland.

One other striking difference, however, is that some parts of eastern and southern Africa and the offshore islands became receiving areas for coerced labor, as the Cape Colony had done since the eighteenth century. In the 1780s, the Mascarene islands, then Isle de France and Bourbon (now Mauritius and Réunion) began a similar transition from way-stations on the route to the east to full membership in the plantation complex. Slave imports began to grow, drawn mainly from the African coast around Mozambique and from the island of Madagascar.[12]

After 1808, the slave trade of the Indian Ocean began to taper off in some respects, but a trickle and sometimes more than a trickle of illicit slave trade continued.[13] If the Mascarenes, Madagascar, and Zanzibar are considered to be off-shore Africa—and they should be so considered—these nineteenth-century slave movements were part of a complex pattern of African population movement, partly overland but partly by sea. The chief source of mainland slaves was the hinterland of the east coast from the mouth of the Zambezi to Dar Es-Salaam and inland to Lake Malawi and beyond. Madagascar was both a major source and a major destination in this intra-African slave trade. The other major destinations were the Mascarene sugar plantations, along with the clove plantations on Zanzibar and Pemba and the food-producing plantations on the Kenya coast. A minor current in this trade also led further north to south Arabia and the Persian Gulf.[14]

By the 1830s and 1840s, the sugar industry on Réunion and Mauritius was growing rapidly, and legal slave exports from Africa were hard to find. Both turned to India as a new source of labor. This alternative was comparatively easy for Mauritius, now a British colony, but Réunion had been returned to France. It drew some indentured workers from French Indian posts like Pondichéry, but after 1860 an agreement with Britain permitted Réunion to import 6,000 indentured workers from British India each year.[15] The Réunionais population soon had an Indian majority—as Mauritius had done even earlier in the century.

Mauritius also served as a stepping stone for the extension of Indian labor migration to South Africa. Britain annexed Natal in 1845. As early as 1847, would-be planters there introduced sugar cane from Mauritius, but they believed they had a labor problem. Local Africans could not be lured into estate labor—not, at least, for the wages planters were willing to pay. After 1860, the government of Natal worked out an indentured-labor agreement with the Indian government. The normal contract stipulated that the workers could return to India free of charge when their time was up, but few actually did return. The result was a flow of coerced labor large enough to create an Indian community in coastal Natal. That community grew to just under a million people, or about 2 percent of the present South African population.[16]

Other Indians also moved to the East African mainland. In the 1890s, the government of the East African Protectorate turned to India for contract labor to build the projected railway from Mombasa to Lake Victoria. In all, some 19,000 Indians worked on the railway, and about half of them returned to India. Many of the rest died, but the remainder settled in Kenya.[17]

The South African mining industry also toyed with the prospect of Asian labor. Between 1903 and 1907, mine owners on the Witwatersrand worked out a scheme to import Chinese miners on three-year contracts. They brought some 97,000 Chinese to South Africa under this arrangement, but it attracted such unfavorable notice in Britain that it had to be abandoned. In this case, almost all of those who survived were repatriated.[18]

Asian trade diasporas had brought Asian visitors to Africa for many centuries, but the numbers were too small to qualify as a migration until the nineteenth century, when Indian commercial activity in East Africa increased with the rising value of Indian Ocean trade. Indian capital helped to finance the clove plantations of Zanzibar and Pemba and the Afro-Arab trade to the interior. Indian entrepreneurs came as individuals or small groups to participate in the growing trade of East Africa, Madagascar, and the Mascarene Islands. A Zanzibar Indian firm had, indeed, organized the trade in indentured workers to build the Uganda railway. At the end of the colonial period in eastern tropical Africa, Indians were more numerous than the European colonizers almost everywhere. In Kenya at independence, they were 3 percent of the population, as against only 1 percent for settlers from Europe. Similar but somewhat smaller groups of Chinese were also active on all of the Indian Ocean coasts.

African Migration in the Twentieth Century

With the consolidation of European colonial rule over Africa in the first decades of this century, the previous patterns of population movement—largely that of enslaved people being moved to new homes—began to change. With gradual emancipation, some people were able to return to their original homes, though most of them settled down where they already lived, often under pressure from the colonial governments not to move.[19]

At the same time, colonial governments wanted other population movement for the sake of economic development. The offer of wages was one incentive, but many colonial governments used forced labor for public employment, forced labor for private European firms, or less overt incentives like heavy direct taxation that could only be met with the proceeds of wage labor.

Together, these incentives drew workers toward the port towns like Lagos, Accra, Dakar, or Mombasa—or toward centers of development under European initiative in plantation agriculture, mining, or railway building. African initiative created other growth centers, like the Gold Coast cocoa farms, Senegalese and Nigerian peanuts, or Ugandan cotton farming. Labor migration often began with the movement of young men on a short-term basis, often seasonal. This temporary or circulatory labor migration was common to most developing economies in recent centuries. It was an introductory phase that died out as workers settled down where jobs were, sent for their families, or married local women. Labor stabilization was slower in tropical Africa than it was elsewhere, partly because economic development there was comparatively weak.

Some circulatory labor existed throughout tropical Africa. In 1960, for example, more than 600,000 people in tropical Africa crossed international frontiers each year in search of work, a significant part of the total wage-labor force. In the savanna country of West Africa, many of these migrants moved back and forth in response to natural conditions. A dry season of six months or more meant that many were seasonally underemployed. It was easy and natural for people from Burkina Faso to move each dry season to the cocoa farms of Ghana or Côte d'Ivoire, where labor was needed at that time of the year, returning north when they could be useful again on their own farms.[20] Over recent decades, many of these circulatory migrants have tended to settle down as stabilized labor in cities and mining areas, though the pattern of continued drift toward centers of economic growth has by no means stopped.

Over the whole colonial and post-colonial periods, the drift of population in West Africa has been from north to south, out of the savanna country toward the forest and coastal regions, where economic development was concentrated. Export agriculture was more important in the forest zone than in the savanna. Whatever industrial development took place tended to be located in or near the ports or other southern centers, and all important petroleum finds were near the coast.

The desert-edge drought that began in the 1960s and continued with only occasional remissions into the 1980s also pushed people southward, as the chamber of the demographic pump that had filled with people during the relatively humid years of the early century was emptied toward the south. Those forced south by a series of dry years often found no incentive to return home when conditions improved. Similar considerations apply to flight from drought in the horn of Africa, though the flight from drought in that part of the world is too intertwined with flight from oppression or fear of oppression to be easily disentangled.

North Africa also began the colonial period with patterns of circulatory labor gradually tending toward stabilization in major urban centers like Cairo, Tunis, Algiers, or Casablanca. In Egypt in particular, low-Nile cultivation was gradually introduced beginning in the nineteenth century with new systems of dams and canals. One result was a broad redistribution of people throughout the countryside. Agricultural change in the Maghrib also brought about redistributions of people, some of which were permanent, though the workers sometimes still moved on a temporary basis only. Particular communities, like the Mozabites of certain oases in southern Algeria, made an important series of cultural adjustments so that they could send young men to the coastal cities for a few years at a time and still have them return to the home community.[21] Other Algerians, however, began as early as the 1930s looking for work in France and elsewhere in Europe, beginning a drift that has continued and grown ever since.

Oscillating Labor in South Africa

South Africa was different. It had the fastest rate of industrialization and economic growth in Africa, but successive South African governments and industries tried to prevent labor stabilization, preferring a system of oscillating or circulatory labor.[22] South African gold mining firms began continuous recruiting of short-term workers as early as the 1890s. They set up a single labor-recruiting agency to attract labor from beyond the South African frontiers. By 1910, the annual number of recruits had already reached 100,000, almost all on short-term contracts, and non-South Africans were already more than half that number.

Between 1913 and 1923, the customary pattern got the support of law. The South African cities and the principal farming areas were declared to be "white man's country," where Africans were only permitted, in theory, under special circumstances and only as temporary sojourners. They were supposed to have permanent homes in the "reserves" set aside for them. In towns or near the mines, they were supposed to live in racially segregated "locations."

The reserves, however, were only 12 percent of South African territory, and that the least developed part. The reserves could not support the African population. South African workers had begun seeking urban employment even before the reserves were created by the Land Act of 1913, and population growth made labor migration even more necessary. Increasingly, men had to leave for work in other parts of South Africa, often leaving their families behind. When the worker's contract expired, usually at the end of a year, he was no longer permitted to stay in the cities; and his family needed his labor in any case to help with chores that went undone during his absence. After a time, however, the need for cash income forced men to return to the mines or European-owned farms. By 1951, at any moment more than a half-million Africans from the reserves were absent on migratory labor in "white" South Africa, representing about 40 percent of all males between the ages of 15 and 65.[23]

Politics and Migration

Many recent patterns of African migration began in the early colonial period and continued with little change into the post-colonial. Political influence on migration, however, has changed drastically. The colonial powers paid comparatively little attention to Africans crossing colonial frontiers, even though they tried to be strict about the movement of Europeans. Here and there, Africans would tend to leave a colonial state they thought was oppressive for better conditions elsewhere, if such conditions were available. People tended, for example, to drift from Mozambique into Nyasaland from time to time during the colonial period—or into the northern Gold Coast from adjacent regions of Upper Volta, if only because of French forced labor and forced military recruitment. But population movements of this kind were tiny compared to the massive displacement in search of employment. In 1960, the approximate end of the colonial period, the only sizable body of refugees were a few hundred thousand Algerians who took refuge in Tunisia during the Algerian war for independence.

The number has been climbing ever since, whatever the basis of calculation. And refugees are notoriously difficult to define. It is hard to tell a political refugee from someone who believes economic conditions have become intolerable. Some authorities, like the United Nations High Commission on Refugees (UNHCR), count only refugees who cross national boundaries. Others also count those who are displaced within their home country. The UNHCR has kept track of refugees since the post-war years. Their count began with virtually none in the 1950s, rising to 400,000 refugees in all parts of Africa by 1964, to more than 1,000,000 by 1970. After a small drop in the early 1970s, the United States Committee for refugees counted more than 3,500,000 in 1981. The latest figures from the UNHCR, those for 1990, are on the order of two million for all of Africa,[24] but they are only for those who move across international frontiers. A recent issue of *The Economist* worked up some figures for the southern Sudan alone, estimating that three million southern Sudanese, or half the population have been forced to leave their homes, whether for other countries or within the Sudan. About two million southerners had left for northern Sudan, 600,000 were displaced within southern Sudan, while 400,000 are in refugee camps in Uganda, Zaire, Kenya, Ethiopia, and the Central African Republic.[25] The *Washington Post* for March 6, 1994 estimated two million refugees from Liberia in neighboring countries and within Liberia itself. The civil wars just ending in Mozambique and still raging in Angola must have generated at least another million, and recent fighting in Rwanda and Burundi would add still more. The present total therefore appears to be in the range of six to eight million people.

Ethnic conflict is the most general cause of the current African refugee problem, though ethnic conflict is probably no more serious in Africa than anywhere else. Beyond ethnic rivalries is the fact that post-colonial African states have not been strong enough to suppress these antagonisms. The parallel with Yugoslavia comes to mind. Ethnic conflict was there all along; it only appeared in the present disastrous form when the former Yugoslavia came apart, leaving no higher authority to settle differences. The Ethiopian state collapsed in a similar way beginning in 1974, and both superpowers turned up willing to arm whatever clients they could find to oppose the influence of the other. The collapse of Somalia followed, after the two superpowers had armed all and sundry. The fall of the Portuguese empire after 1975 released similar ethnic conflicts. This time, South Africa joined the superpowers in arming the potential antagonists, so as to turn ethnic conflict into major and disastrous civil wars in both Angola and Mozambique. The long-standing civil war in the Sudan has been exacerbated in the same way by the intervention of Iran and Libya.

It is still impossible to predict an outcome of these or any similar conflicts, but it seems certain that the ethnic map (if not the political map) will be drastically changed. The longer refugees are forced to live abroad, the less likely they will be able to go "home." The earliest wave of the Tutsi and Hutu refugees from Rwanda and Burundi respectively occurred in 1962-63. After thirty years, a predictable majority of the refugee communities in Kenya or Uganda were born in exile, and they probably have small incentive to return.

The Post-War Migration to the Most Developed World

As I mentioned at the beginning of this lecture, one of the major changes in world migration patterns was the heavy flow of migrants from the tropical and less-developed world toward the centers of world economic development. The underlying dynamic is familiar. Most of the tropical world has had a rate

41

of population growth at around 2.5 percent per year or more, while population growth rates in the developed world have tended toward zero. The rates of economic growth have often been the reverse.

Africans were not always the leading players in these new movements, but they were certainly participants. North Africans were among the most active, reversing the colonial flow of people across the Mediterranean. The Algerian population in the mid-1980s was about 22 million, but a million Algerians were temporary residents abroad, working mainly in France. Just before independence, the European settler population of Algeria had been about a million people, and nearly all returned to France (even though a majority had come from somewhere else). The recent population of Morocco was about 23 million, of whom just over 60,000 were resident foreigners, but more than one million Moroccans were living abroad, mainly in Europe as migrant workers.[26] The Tunisian situation was similar.

By the late 1980s, African immigration was also significant in Europe outside of France. In 1985, Africans made up more than 10 percent of all immigrants into Belgium and the Netherlands. Some of these were circulatory labor migrants, but not all of them. Many brought their families and settled in Europe. In the late 1980s, Belgium, West Germany, the Netherlands, and Switzerland reported the number of arrivals and departures by source and destination, and arrivals from Africa exceeded departures by about 50 percent.[27]

The United States has also shared in this new migration out of Africa. The American Immigration and Naturalization Service reports, by country of origin arrivals who intend to become American residents. The annual number of immigrants from Africa rose ten-fold between the decade of the 1960s and 1990. Though Africans were still only 2.3 percent of all immigrants, the total of 36 thousand Africans arriving in 1990[28] was a good deal higher than the annual average arrivals from Africa in the era of the slave trade.

Summary

In conclusion, then, we have that people migrated within Africa and into and out of Africa for many different reasons, but the oldest and most consistent was the possession of some technological advantage—including the ability to use an occupational niche that was not already filled. We have seen this in the case of Malagasy seafarers, the Arabian camel herders, or the early agricultural skills of the Bantu-speaking migrants.

Commercial skills also counted, like those of small groups who moved along the trade routes, though the numbers involved in early trade diasporas were probably too small to count as a real migration. In the nineteenth century, however, commercial opportunities increased with the industrialization of Japan and the West. Communities with developed commercial skills could move more freely into less commercially developed regions like sub-Saharan Africa.

Military power was another kind of technological edge that led to migration in Africa. It lay behind some of the Arabian migrations across North Africa, behind the spread of the various off-shoots of the Mfecane in southern Africa, behind the spread of the Afrikaners north from the Cape, and in a more distant way behind the smaller migrations that followed colonial conquest.

Another kind of migration was coerced in a different way, on the incentive of those who wanted the services of the migrants. The pull of the plantation complex expressed through the slave trade was a major factor in African history. Epidemiological factors reinforced the movement—on both sides of the tropical Atlantic—and socio-political conditions in Africa made recruitment of slaves there easier than it might have been in other societies.

By the eighteenth century and on into the nineteenth, Africa itself moved from the sending to the receiving end of this form of migration, with the movement of slaves from Indonesia, India, and Madagascar into the Cape Colony—and later of indentured Indian and Chinese workers into the sugar plantations of the Mascarene Islands and Natal, the Rand gold fields, and Kenyan railway construction.

A second kind of coerced migration was that of refugees. The initiative was often their own, but only because fear for their safety led them to flee.

The final category is the migration of individuals, moving on their own initiative to seek their fortune, not so much because they had skills to offer, but because they were willing to take work that members of more developed economies avoided. The movement out of Africa in the past forty years has been partly in this pattern, partly the brain-drain of the skilled and educated. In any event, the initiative was that of the migrants themselves, encouraged by lop-sided economic growth centered in the north, combined with lop-sided population growth centered in the south.

Notes to Lecture II

1. The end of the Atlantic slave trade has been treated at enormous length and from many points of view. Some of these can be surveyed by consulting Eric Williams, *Capitalism and Slavery* (Chapel Hill: University of North Carolina Press, 1944); Seymour Drescher, *Econocide: British Slavery in the Era of Abolition* (Pittsburgh: University of Pittsburgh Press, 1977); Barbara Solow and Stanley Engerman, *British Capitalism and Caribbean Slavery: The Legacy of Eric Williams* (New York: Cambridge University Press, 1988).

2. The literature about these migrations is large and increasing: Hugh Tinker, *A New System of Slavery: The Export of Indian Labour Overseas 1830-1920* (London: Oxford University Press, 1974); Pieter C. Emmer (Ed.), *Colonialism and Migration: Indentured Labour Before and After Slavery* (Dordrecht: Nijhoff, 1986); Shula Marks and Peter Richardson (Eds.), *Studies in International Labour Migration: Historical Perspectives* (London: Macmillan, 1984); David Northrup, *Indentured Labor in the Age of Imperialism, 1838-1914* (New York: Cambridge University Press, forthcoming); Pieter C. Emmer (Ed.), *European Expansion and Migration: Essays on the Intercontinental Migration from Africa, Asia, and Europe* (Oxford: Berg, 1992).

3. Northrup, *Indentured Labor*, Ch. 2, n. 2. See also P. D. Curtin, "Migration in the Tropical World," in Virginia Yans-McLaughlin, *Immigration Reconsidered: History, Sociology, and Politics* (New York: Oxford University Press, 1990), 21-36.

4. Philip D. Curtin, *Cross-Cultural Trade in World History* (New York: Cambridge University Press, 1984), 136-57.

5. Leonard Thompson, *A History of South Africa* (New Haven: Yale University Press, 1990), 33-45.

6. Robert C.-H. Shell, *Children of Bondage* (Middletown, CT: Wesleyan University Press, 1994).

7. United Nations, Department of Economic and Social Affairs, *Economic Survey of Africa Since 1950* (New York, 1959), 13.
8. UN, *Economic Survey of Africa Since 1950*, 13.
9. John H. Hanson,"Islam, Migration and the Political Economy of Meaning: *Fergo Nioro* from the Senegal River Valley, 1862-1890," *Journal of African History*, 35 (1994), 37-60.
10. Richard L. Roberts, *Warriors, Merchants, and Slaves: The State and the Economy in the Middle Niger Valley, 1700-1914* (Stanford: Stanford University Press, 1987); Patrick Manning, "Slavery and the Slave Trade in Colonial Africa," *Journal of African History*, 32 (1990), 235-40; Paul E. Lovejoy, "The Impact of the Atlantic Slave Trade on Africa: A Review of the Literature," *Journal of African History*, 30 (1989), 365-94; Suzanne Miers and Richard Roberts (Eds.), *The End of Slavery in Africa* (Madison: University of Wisconsin Press, 1989).
11. Janet J. Ewald, "The Nile Valley System and the Red Sea Slave Trade 1820-1880," *Slavery & Abolition*, 9 (1988), 72-92; "Slavery in Africa and the Slave Trade from Africa," *American Historical Review*, 97 (1992), 465-85.
12. Burton Benedict, "Slavery and Indenture in Mauritius and Seychelles" in James L. Watson (Ed.), *Asian and African Systems of Slavery* (Berkeley: University of California Press, 1980), 125-68.
13. Gwyn Campbell, "The East African Slave Trade, 1861-1895," *International Journal of African Historical Studies*, 22 (1989), 1-26.
14. Esmond Bradley Martin and T.C.I. Ryan, "Estimating Slave Imports to the Mascarenes: An Essay in Methodology," *Hekima: Journal of Humanities and Social Sciences* [Nairobi], No. 2 (December 1982), 66-81; William Gervase Clarence-Smith (Ed.), *The Economics of the Indian Ocean Slave Trade in the Nineteenth Century* (London: Frank Cass, 1989); Campbell, "The East African Slave Trade"; and "The State and Pre-Colonial Demographic History: The Case of Nineteenth-Century Madagascar," *Journal of African History,* 32 (1991), 415-45; Abdul Sheriff, *Slaves, Spices and Ivory in Zanzibar: Integration of an East African Commercial*

Empire into the World Economy, 1770-1873 (London: James Currey, 1987).

15. Tinker, *New System of Slavery*, 65, 95, 99.

16. Thompson, *History of South Africa*, 243.

17. Robert G. Gregory, *India and East Africa: A History of Race Relations within the British Empire, 1890-1939* (Oxford: Clarendon Press, 1971); Tinker, *New System of Slavery,* 278.

18. Peter Richardson, "Chinese Indentured Labour in the Transvaal Gold Mining Industry, 1904-1910," in Kay Saunders (Ed.), *Indentured Labour in the British Empire 1834-1920* (London and Canberra: Croom Helm, 1984), 260-90, esp. 266 ff.

19. See, for example, Paul E. Lovejoy and Jan S. Hogendorn, *Slow Death for Slavery: The Course of Abolition in Northern Nigeria, 1897-1936* (Cambridge: Cambridge University Press, 1993), and Miers and Roberts, *End of Slavery in Africa.*

20. See, for example, Dennis D. Cordell, Joel Gregory, and Victor Piché, *Hoe and Wage: A Social History of a Circulatory Migration System in West Africa* (Boulder: Westview, 1994); John A. Arthur, "International Labor Migration Patterns in West Africa," *African Studies Review*, 34 (1991), 65-87.

21. Donald C. Holsinger, "Migration, Commerce, and Community: The Mizabis in Eighteenth- and Nineteenth-Century Algeria," *Journal of African History*, 21 (1980), 61-74.

22. Francis Wilson, *Labour in the South African Gold Mines, 1911-1969* (Cambridge: Cambridge University Press, 1972); Sharon Stichter, *Migrant Laborers* (New York: Cambridge University Press, 1985); Philip D. Curtin, "Postwar Migrations in Sub-Saharan Africa," in William H. McNeill and Ruth Adams, *Human Migration: Patterns and Policies* (Bloomington: Indiana University Press, 1976) 188-98.

23. Curtin, "Postwar Migrations," 191.

24. United Nations, General Assembly, 47th session, "Report of the United Nations High Commission for Refugees," Official Records, Supplement no. 12 (A/46/12), 17-22. See also Aristide R. Zolberg, Astri Sulurke, and Serio Aguayo, *Escape from Violence: Conflict and the Refugee Crisis in*

the Developing World (New York: Oxford University Press, 1989), 37-40.

25. *The Economist*, 330 (February 12, 1994), 39-40.
26. Trevor Mostyn (Ed.), *Cambridge Encyclopedia of the Middle East and North Africa* (Cambridge: Cambridge University Press, 1988), 302, 388.
27. United Nations, *Demographic Yearbook 1989*, 576-98.
28. *Statistical Abstract of the United States 1992*, 10.

PHILIP D. CURTIN

Professor Curtin was born in Philadelphia, Pennsylvania, on May 22, 1922, but spent most of his youth in West Virginia. He received his B.A. degree in 1948 from Swarthmore College, where he was elected to Phi Beta Kappa. he received his M.S. and Ph.D. from Harvard in 1949 and 1953, respectively.

Currently Herbert Baxter Adams Professor of History at Johns Hopkins University, he has also taught at Swarthmore College, the University of Wisconsin, the University of Hawaii, and the University of Minnesota.

Professor Curtin has been extremely active in professional organizations. He was president of the American Historical Association in 1983 and a member of the council for 1967-71. He was president of the African Studies Association for 1970-71 and held numerous other offices with the Association over the years. Among the other organizations for which he has held office are the American Council of Learned Societies, the Economic History Association, the Library of Congress, and the World History Association. He has served on the editorial boards of nine scholarly journals including the *American Historical Review.*

Among the many awards and prizes he has received are the following: Ford Fellowship, Guggenheim Fellowship, national Endowment for the Humanities Fellowship, McArthur Prize Fellowship, the Robert Livingston Schuyler Prize, Welch Medal from the American Association for the History of Medicine, and the Distinguished Africanist Award.

Professor Curtin has written or edited fifteen books and over fifty articles, among them:

> *The Atlantic Slave Trade: A Census* (Madison: University of Wisconsin Press, 1969).
>
> *Cross-Cultural Trade in World History* (Cambridge: Cambridge University Press, 1984).
>
> *Death by Migration* (Cambridge: Cambridge University Press, 1989).
>
> *The Rise and Fall of the Plantation Complex: Essay in Atlantic History* (Cambridge: Cambridge University Press, 1989).

Previous
CHARLES EDMONDSON HISTORICAL LECTURERS

Paul K. Conkin, University of Wisconsin, 1977–1978: "American Christianity in Crisis: Religious Rationalism and Darwinism"

*Walter LaFeber, Cornell University, 1979–1980: "The Third Cold War: Kissinger Years and Carter Years"

*Martin E. Marty, University of Chicago, 1980–1981: "Religious Crises in Modern America: Modernism and Fundamentalism"

**William H. McNeill, University of Chicago, 1981–1982: "The Great Frontier: Freedom and Hierarchy in Modern Times"

Robert L. Heilbroner, The New School for Social Research, 1982–1983: "Capitalism in Transition: The Twentieth Century"

C. Vann Woodward, Yale University, emeritus, 1983–1984: "Continuing Themes in Southern History: The Strange Career of Jim Crow, 1954–1984; The Burden of Southern History, 1952–1984"

*William E. Leuchtenburg, University of North Carolina, Chapel Hill, 1984–1985: "The 1984 Presidential Election in Historical Perspective: From Civil War to the New Deal; From Franklin Roosevelt to Ronald Reagan"

Peter Gay, Yale University, 1985–1986: "Aggression: Toward a Theory of Aggression; Humor: Aggression at Work"

*Gordon S. Wood, Brown University, 1986–1987: "The Making of the Constitution"

Gerda Lerner, University of Wisconsin, Madison, 1987–1988: "Sex and Class: A Revisionist Perspective"

*Robert Darnton, Princeton University, 1988-1989: "What was Revolutionary about the French Revolution?"

*Stephen B. Oates, University of Massachusetts, Amherst, 1989-1990: "Biography as History"

*Dan T. Carter, Emory University, 1990-1991: "George Wallace, Richard Nixon, and the Transformation of American Politics"

*Geoffrey Alan Hosking, University of London, 1991-1992: "Empire and Nation in Russian History"

*Nell Irvin Painter, Princeton University, 1992-1993: "Soul Murder and Slavery"

*Printed copies are available from the Baylor University Press.
**Printed copies are available from the Princeton University Press.